FIX IT QUICK
CHINESE

Publications International, Ltd.

Favorite Brand Name Recipes at www.fbnr.com

Pictured on the front cover *(clockwise from top left):* Chicken Chow Mein *(page 103),* Chinese Pork & Vegetable Stir-Fry *(page 62),* Chicken with Lychees *(page 66)* and Mongolian Vegetables *(page 40).*

Pictured on the back cover: Seared Asian Steak Salad *(page 120).*

ISBN-13: 978-1-4127-2732-7
ISBN-10: 1-4127-2732-4

Library of Congress Control Number: 2007936264

Manufactured in China.

8 7 6 5 4 3 2 1

Microwave Cooking: Microwave ovens vary in wattage. Use the cooking times as guidelines and check for doneness before adding more time.

Preparation/Cooking Times: Preparation times are based on the approximate amount of time required to assemble the recipe before cooking, baking, chilling or serving. These times include preparation steps such as measuring, chopping and mixing. The fact that some preparations and cooking can be done simultaneously is taken into account. Preparation of optional ingredients and serving suggestions is not included.

table of contents

chinatown stuffed mushrooms

24 large mushrooms (about 1 pound)
½ pound ground turkey
1 clove garlic, minced
¼ cup dry bread crumbs
¼ cup thinly sliced green onions
3 tablespoons soy sauce, divided
1 egg white, lightly beaten
1 teaspoon minced fresh ginger
⅛ teaspoon red pepper flakes (optional)

1. Remove stems from mushrooms; finely chop enough stems to equal 1 cup. Cook turkey, chopped mushroom stems and garlic in medium skillet over medium-high heat until turkey is no longer pink, stirring to break up meat. Drain fat. Stir in bread crumbs, green onions, 2 tablespoons soy sauce, egg white, ginger and pepper flakes, if desired; mix well.

2. Preheat broiler. Line broiler pan with foil; insert broiler rack. Coat broiler rack with nonstick cooking spray.

3. Brush mushroom caps lightly with remaining 1 tablespoon soy sauce; spoon about 2 teaspoons stuffing into each mushroom cap.* Place stuffed mushrooms on prepared broiler rack. Broil 4 to 5 inches from heat 5 to 6 minutes or until heated through.   *Makes 24 appetizers*

*Mushrooms can be made ahead to this point; cover and refrigerate up to 24 hours. Add 1 to 2 minutes to broiling time for chilled mushrooms.

chinatown stuffed mushrooms

hoisin-orange chicken wraps

½ teaspoon grated orange peel
¼ cup orange juice
¼ cup hoisin sauce
8 whole Boston lettuce leaves
2 cups shredded coleslaw mix
2 cups diced cooked chicken (about 8 ounces)
   Black pepper (optional)

Combine orange peel, orange juice and hoisin sauce in small bowl. Arrange lettuce leaves on large serving platter. Place ¼ cup coleslaw, ¼ cup chicken and 1 tablespoon hoisin mixture on each leaf. Sprinkle with pepper, if desired. Fold lettuce over to create wraps. *Makes 8 wraps*

chinese crab & cucumber salad

1 large cucumber, peeled
12 ounces crabmeat (fresh, pasteurized or thawed frozen), flaked
½ red bell pepper, diced
½ cup mayonnaise
3 tablespoons soy sauce
1 tablespoon sesame oil
1 teaspoon ground ginger
½ pound bean sprouts
1 tablespoon sesame seeds, toasted
   Fresh chives, cut into 1-inch pieces

Cut cucumber in half lengthwise; scoop out seeds. Cut cucumber into bite-size pieces. Combine cucumber, crabmeat and bell pepper in large bowl. Blend mayonnaise, soy sauce, sesame oil and ginger in small bowl. Add to crabmeat mixture; toss to mix well. Refrigerate 1 hour to allow flavors to blend. To serve, arrange bean sprouts on individual serving plates. Spoon crabmeat mixture on top; sprinkle with sesame seeds and chives. *Makes 8 servings*

hoisin-orange chicken wraps

hot and sour soup

1 package (1 ounce) dried shiitake mushrooms
4 ounces firm tofu, drained
4 cups chicken broth
3 tablespoons white vinegar
2 tablespoons soy sauce
½ to 1 teaspoon hot chili oil
¼ teaspoon white pepper
1 cup shredded cooked pork, chicken or turkey
½ cup drained canned bamboo shoots, cut into thin strips
3 tablespoons water
2 tablespoons cornstarch
1 egg white, lightly beaten
¼ cup thinly sliced green onions or chopped fresh cilantro
1 teaspoon dark sesame oil

1. Place mushrooms in small bowl; cover with warm water. Soak 20 minutes to soften. Drain; squeeze out excess water. Discard stems; slice caps. Press tofu lightly between paper towels; cut into ½-inch squares or triangles.

2. Combine broth, vinegar, soy sauce, chili oil and pepper in medium saucepan. Bring to a boil over high heat. Reduce heat to medium. Simmer 2 minutes.

3. Stir in mushrooms, tofu, pork and bamboo shoots; heat through.

4. Blend water into cornstarch in small bowl until smooth. Stir into soup. Cook and stir 4 minutes or until soup boils and thickens.

5. Remove from heat. Stirring constantly in one direction, slowly pour egg white in thin stream into soup. Stir in green onions and sesame oil. Ladle into soup bowls. *Makes 4 to 6 servings*

hot and sour soup

roasted shanghai pepper salad

      1 jar (14 to 15 ounces) roasted red and/or yellow peppers
  1½ tablespoons soy sauce
      1 tablespoon rice vinegar
      1 tablespoon dark sesame oil
      2 teaspoons honey
      1 clove garlic, minced
        Romaine lettuce or spinach leaves
      2 tablespoons coarsely chopped fresh cilantro

1. Drain and rinse peppers; pat dry with paper towels. Cut peppers lengthwise into ½-inch strips; place in small bowl.

2. Combine soy sauce, vinegar, sesame oil, honey and garlic; mix well. Pour over peppers; cover and refrigerate at least 2 hours. Serve over lettuce leaves. Sprinkle with cilantro.   *Makes 4 servings*

portobello mushrooms sesame

      4 large portobello mushrooms
      2 tablespoons sweet rice wine
      2 tablespoons soy sauce
      2 cloves garlic, minced
      1 teaspoon dark sesame oil

1. Prepare grill for direct grilling.

2. Remove and discard stems from mushrooms. Combine rice wine, soy sauce, garlic and sesame oil in small bowl.

3. Brush both sides of mushroom caps with soy sauce mixture. Grill with cap sides up, covered, over medium coals 3 to 4 minutes. Brush tops with soy sauce mixture; turn and grill 2 minutes more or until mushrooms have grill marks. Turn again; grill, basting frequently, 4 to 5 minutes or until tender. Cut diagonally into ½-inch-thick slices.   *Makes 4 servings*

roasted shanghai pepper salad

summer szechuan tofu salad

¼ cup soy sauce
1 tablespoon vegetable oil
1 tablespoon dark sesame oil
1 teaspoon minced fresh ginger
½ teaspoon hot pepper sauce or to taste
1 package extra-firm tofu
4 cups baby spinach leaves
4 cups sliced napa cabbage or romaine lettuce leaves
2 cups diagonally halved sugar snap peas or snow peas
1 cup matchstick-size carrots
1 cup fresh bean sprouts
¼ cup dry-roasted peanuts or toasted slivered almonds
  Chopped cilantro or green onions (optional)

1. Combine soy sauce, vegetable oil, sesame oil, ginger and hot pepper sauce in small bowl. Drain tofu and place between 2 paper towels. Press lightly to drain excess water from tofu. Cut tofu into 1-inch cubes. Place in shallow dish. Drizzle 2 tablespoons soy sauce mixture over tofu cubes. Set aside.

2. Combine spinach, cabbage, sugar snap peas, carrots and bean sprouts in large bowl. Add remaining soy sauce mixture. Toss well. Transfer to plates. Top with tofu, peanuts and cilantro, if desired. *Makes 4 servings*

chinese pork salad

1 pound pork strips
½ cup Oriental stir-fry sauce
½ red onion, peeled and thinly sliced
2 packages (10 ounces each) frozen snow peas, thawed and drained
1 can (8 ounces) mandarin oranges, drained
1 can (3 ounces) chow mein noodles

Marinate pork in stir-fry sauce. In large nonstick skillet, stir-fry pork and onion over medium-high heat 4 to 5 minutes. In large bowl, toss pork mixture together with remaining ingredients. *Makes 4 servings*

Prep Time: 5 minutes
Cook Time: 5 minutes

Favorite recipe from **National Pork Board**

chilled shrimp in chinese mustard sauce

1 cup water
½ cup dry white wine
2 tablespoons soy sauce
½ teaspoon Szechuan pepper or whole black peppercorns
1 pound raw large shrimp, peeled and deveined
¼ cup prepared sweet and sour sauce
2 teaspoons hot Chinese mustard

1. Combine water, wine, soy sauce and pepper in medium saucepan. Bring to a boil over high heat. Add shrimp; reduce heat to medium. Cover and simmer 2 to 3 minutes or until shrimp are opaque and cooked through. Drain well. Cover and refrigerate until chilled.*

2. Combine sweet and sour sauce and mustard in small bowl; mix well. Serve with shrimp. *Makes 6 servings*

*Shrimp can be made ahead to this point; cover and refrigerate for up to 1 day.

Substitution: If you are unable to find hot Chinese mustard or simply want a sauce with less heat, substitute a spicy brown or Dijon mustard.

sausage filled wontons

1 pound BOB EVANS® Original Recipe Roll Sausage
¼ cup chopped onion
½ cup (2 ounces) shredded American cheese
3 ounces cream cheese
½ teaspoon dried marjoram leaves
¼ teaspoon dried tarragon leaves
30 wonton wrappers
   Vegetable oil
   Dipping sauce, such as plum sauce or sweet and sour sauce (optional)

To prepare filling, crumble sausage into large skillet. Add onion. Cook over medium heat until sausage is browned, stirring occasionally. Remove from heat; drain off any drippings. Stir in next 4 ingredients. Mix until cheeses melt. Lightly dampen 1 wonton wrapper by dipping your finger in water and wiping all the edges, making ¼-inch border around square. (To keep wrappers from drying, cover remaining wrappers with damp kitchen towel while working.) Place rounded teaspoonful sausage mixture in the middle of wrapper. Fold wrapper over filling to form triangle, sealing edges and removing any air bubbles. Repeat with remaining wrappers and filling.

Heat 4 inches oil in deep fryer or heavy large saucepan to 350°F; fry wontons, a few at a time, until golden brown. Remove with slotted spoon; drain on paper towels. Reheat oil between batches. Serve hot with dipping sauce, if desired. Refrigerate leftovers.   *Makes 30 appetizers*

quick tip

Wonton wrappers, sometimes called wonton skins, can be purchased in the refrigerated produce department or in the frozen foods section of most supermarkets. These paper-thin pieces of dough are made from flour, water, eggs and salt. You can often choose between square or round wrappers. They are used to make wontons for soup, egg rolls and many other Asian preparations.

sausage filled wontons

chinese chicken salad

3 tablespoons peanut or vegetable oil
3 tablespoons rice vinegar
2 tablespoons soy sauce
1 tablespoon honey
1 teaspoon minced fresh ginger
1 teaspoon dark sesame oil
1 clove garlic, minced
¼ teaspoon red pepper flakes
4 cups chopped cooked chicken or turkey
4 cups packed shredded napa cabbage or romaine lettuce
1 cup shredded carrots
½ cup thinly sliced green onions
1 can (5 ounces) chow mein noodles (optional)
¼ cup chopped cashews or peanuts
   Carrot curls and green onions (optional)

1. For dressing, combine peanut oil, vinegar, soy sauce, honey, ginger, sesame oil, garlic and red pepper flakes in small jar with tight-fitting lid; shake well.

2. Place chicken in large bowl. Pour dressing over chicken; toss to coat.*

3. Add cabbage, shredded carrots and sliced green onions to bowl; toss well to coat. Serve over chow mein noodles, if desired. Sprinkle with cashews and garnish with carrot curls and additional green onions.

Makes 4 to 6 servings (about 8 cups salad)

Salad may be made ahead to this point; cover and refrigerate chicken mixture until ready to serve.

chinese chicken salad

shantung twin mushroom soup

1 package (1 ounce) dried shiitake mushrooms
2 teaspoons vegetable oil
1 large onion, coarsely chopped
2 cloves garlic, minced
2 cups sliced fresh button mushrooms
2 cans (about 14 ounces each) reduced-sodium chicken broth
2 ounces cooked ham, cut into thin slivers
½ cup thinly sliced green onions
1 tablespoon soy sauce
1 tablespoon dry sherry
1 tablespoon cornstarch

1. Place dried mushrooms in small bowl; cover with warm water. Soak 20 minutes to soften. Drain; squeeze out excess water. Discard stems; slice caps.

2. Heat oil in large saucepan over medium heat. Add chopped onion and garlic; cook 1 minute. Add dried and fresh mushrooms; cook 4 minutes, stirring occasionally.

3. Add broth; bring to a boil over high heat. Reduce heat to medium; simmer, covered, 15 minutes.

4. Stir in ham and green onions; heat through. Blend soy sauce and sherry into cornstarch in small bowl until smooth; stir into soup. Cook 2 minutes or until soup is thickened, stirring occasionally. *Makes 6 servings*

shantung twin mushroom soup

asian brown rice and peanut salad toss

1½ cups water
¾ cup uncooked brown rice
⅔ cup dry-roasted peanuts
1 can (8 ounces) sliced water chestnuts, drained
1 cup snow peas
½ cup chopped red onion
½ cup chopped green bell pepper
¼ cup dried cranberries or raisins
2 tablespoons cider vinegar
2 tablespoons honey
2 tablespoons soy sauce
¼ teaspoon red pepper flakes

1. Bring water to a boil over high heat in medium saucepan. Stir in rice; return to a boil. Reduce heat; simmer, covered, 30 to 40 minutes or until rice is tender and liquid is absorbed. Rinse rice with cold water; drain well.

2. Meanwhile, place small skillet over medium-high heat. Add peanuts; cook and stir 3 to 4 minutes or until fragrant and beginning to brown. Transfer to large bowl. Stir in water chestnuts, snow peas, onion, bell pepper and cranberries. Stir in rice.

3. Combine vinegar, honey, soy sauce and pepper flakes in small bowl. Add vinegar mixture to rice mixture; toss to coat. *Makes 6 servings*

quick tip

If you have occasion to visit an Asian market, check out the wide variety of soy sauce that is offered. There are not only many different brands, but many different styles as well. You can choose from thick or thin soy sauce, sweet soy sauce, mushroom soy sauce and Chinese black soy sauce among others. `

asian brown rice and peanut salad toss

chinese cabbage salad

6 tablespoons cider vinegar

3 tablespoons sugar

1 tablespoon dark sesame oil

1 teaspoon minced fresh ginger

1 large crisp red apple, diced

1 medium (1 to 1¼ pounds) head green cabbage, shredded, *or* 1 bag (16 ounces) coleslaw mix

⅓ cup golden raisins

2 green onions, thinly sliced

2 tablespoons chopped fresh cilantro

1 tablespoon toasted sesame seeds

1. Combine vinegar, sugar, oil and ginger in large bowl; stir until sugar dissolves. Stir in apple.

2. Add cabbage, raisins, onions, cilantro and sesame seeds; gently stir until well combined.   *Makes 6 servings*

orange-onion salad

1 tablespoon rice vinegar

1 tablespoon soy sauce

2 teaspoons dark sesame oil

1 large navel orange, peeled and sliced

1 small red onion, thinly sliced

Romaine lettuce or spinach leaves

1. Combine vinegar, soy sauce and sesame oil in small bowl.

2. Place orange and onion slices in single layer in shallow baking dish; drizzle with soy sauce mixture. Cover and refrigerate at least 30 minutes or up to 8 hours.

3. Transfer orange and onion slices to lettuce-lined serving platter or individual lettuce-lined dishes; drizzle with juices from dish.

Makes 4 servings

chinese cabbage salad

simple stir-fries

szechuan pork stir-fry over spinach

  2 teaspoons dark sesame oil, divided
¾ cup matchstick-size carrot strips
½ pound lean pork tenderloin, cut into thin strips
  3 cloves garlic, minced
  2 teaspoons minced fresh ginger
¼ to ½ teaspoon red pepper flakes
  1 tablespoon soy sauce
  1 tablespoon rice wine or dry sherry
  2 teaspoons cornstarch
  8 ounces baby spinach
  2 teaspoons sesame seeds, toasted*

To toast sesame seeds, spread in large, dry skillet. Shake skillet over medium-low heat about 3 minutes or until seeds begin to pop and turn golden.

1. Heat 1 teaspoon oil in large nonstick skillet over medium-high heat. Add carrot strips. Cook 3 minutes, stirring occasionally. Add pork, garlic, ginger and red pepper flakes. Stir-fry 3 minutes or until pork is no longer pink. Combine soy sauce, rice wine and cornstarch in small bowl. Add to pork mixture. Stir-fry about 1 minute or until sauce thickens.

2. Heat remaining 1 teaspoon oil in medium saucepan over medium-high heat. Add spinach. Cover and cook 1 minute or until spinach is barely wilted. Transfer spinach to 2 serving plates. Spoon pork mixture over spinach. Top with sesame seeds. *Makes 2 servings*

szechuan pork stir-fry over spinach

stir-fried eggplant and tofu

1 green onion
4 ounces lean ground pork
2 cloves garlic, minced
1 teaspoon minced fresh ginger
½ teaspoon dark sesame oil
4 ounces firm tofu
½ teaspoon cornstarch
½ cup chicken broth
1 pound Asian eggplants
2 tablespoons peanut oil
1 tablespoon soy sauce
1 teaspoon chili garlic sauce
½ teaspoon sugar

1. Mince white part of green onion. Cut green part of onion diagonally into 1½-inch lengths; reserve for garnish.

2. Combine pork, chopped green onion, garlic, ginger and sesame oil in medium bowl.

3. Press tofu between sheets of paper towels. Cut into ½-inch cubes.

4. Stir cornstarch into chicken broth in small bowl; set aside.

5. To prepare eggplants, trim off cap and stem ends; cut lengthwise into quarters, then into 1-inch pieces.

6. Heat peanut oil in wok or large skillet over high heat. Add eggplant; stir-fry 5 to 6 minutes or until tender. Add tofu; stir-fry 1 minute. Remove eggplant and tofu from wok; set aside.

7. Add pork mixture to wok; stir-fry about 2 minutes or until browned. Add soy sauce, chili sauce and sugar; cook and stir until heated through.

8. Return eggplant and tofu to wok. Stir cornstarch mixture; add to wok. Cook and stir until sauce thickens. Garnish with green onion.

Makes 4 servings

stir-fried eggplant and tofu

beef and broccoli

1 pound beef tenderloin steaks
2 teaspoons minced fresh ginger
2 cloves garlic, minced
½ teaspoon vegetable oil
3 cups broccoli florets
¼ cup water
2 tablespoons teriyaki sauce
Hot cooked rice

1. Cut beef crosswise into ⅛-inch-thick slices. Toss beef with ginger and garlic in medium bowl.

2. Heat oil in wok or large nonstick skillet over medium heat. Stir-fry beef in batches 2 to 3 minutes or until beef is barely pink in center. Remove beef from wok.

3. Add broccoli and water to wok; cover and steam 3 to 5 minutes or until broccoli is crisp-tender. Return beef and any accumulated juices to wok. Add teriyaki sauce. Cook until heated through. Serve over rice.

Makes 4 servings

sweet and sour shrimp stir-fry

1 tablespoon dark sesame oil
½ cup thinly sliced celery
¼ cup chopped red bell pepper
¼ cup chopped green onions
½ teaspoon ground ginger
1 teaspoon soy sauce
1 teaspoon lemon juice
1 teaspoon sugar
1 pound medium raw shrimp, peeled

1. Heat oil in wok or large nonstick skillet over medium heat. Add celery, bell pepper, green onions and ginger. Stir-fry 5 to 7 minutes.

2. Add soy sauce, lemon juice and sugar; stir-fry 1 minute. Add shrimp; cook 3 minutes or until shrimp are pink and opaque. *Makes 4 servings*

beef and broccoli

stir-fried pork with green beans and baby corn

¾ **pound pork tenderloin**
1 tablespoon plus 1 teaspoon cornstarch, divided
2 tablespoons soy sauce
1 tablespoon rice wine or dry sherry
1 teaspoon sugar
½ **teaspoon dark sesame oil**
⅓ **cup plus 2 tablespoons water, divided**
2 tablespoons peanut oil, divided
1 pound green beans, cut into 1½-inch pieces
2 cloves garlic, minced
1 teaspoon finely chopped fresh ginger
1 tablespoon black bean sauce
1 can (14 ounces) baby corn, rinsed and drained

1. Slice pork across grain into thin slices; cut slices into ¾-inch strips.

2. Combine 1 teaspoon cornstarch, soy sauce, rice wine, sugar and sesame oil in medium bowl; mix well. Add pork; toss to coat. Set aside to marinate 20 to 30 minutes. Combine remaining 1 tablespoon cornstarch and ⅓ cup water in small bowl; set aside.

3. Heat 1 tablespoon peanut oil in wok or large skillet over high heat. Add green beans; stir-fry about 4 minutes. Add remaining 2 tablespoons water; reduce heat to medium-low. Cover and simmer 10 to 12 minutes or until crisp-tender. Remove from wok; set aside.

4. Heat remaining 1 tablespoon peanut oil in wok over high heat. Add garlic, ginger and pork; stir-fry about 3 minutes or until meat is no longer pink. Add black bean sauce; stir-fry 1 minute.

5. Return green beans to wok. Stir cornstarch mixture; add to wok. Bring to a boil; cook until sauce thickens. Stir in baby corn; heat through.

Makes 4 servings

stir-fried pork with green beans and baby corn

stir-fried catfish with cucumber rice

1 seedless cucumber
1¼ cups water
½ cup uncooked rice
4 green onions, thinly sliced
½ teaspoon white pepper
2 teaspoons canola oil
1 pound catfish fillets, cut into 1-inch chunks
1 teaspoon minced fresh ginger
1 clove garlic, minced
¼ teaspoon dark sesame oil
3 cups snow peas
1 red bell pepper, diced
¼ cup white wine or water
1 tablespoon cornstarch

1. Grate cucumber on medium holes of grater into colander set over bowl; drain.

2. Combine water, rice, cucumber, green onions and white pepper in medium saucepan. Bring to a boil over medium heat. Cover; reduce heat to low. Cook about 20 minutes or until rice is tender and liquid is absorbed.

3. Heat oil in wok or large nonstick skillet over high heat. Add catfish, ginger, garlic and sesame oil. Stir-fry 4 to 5 minutes or until catfish is just cooked. Add snow peas and bell pepper. Cover and cook 4 minutes.

4. Meanwhile, stir wine into cornstarch in small bowl. Pour over catfish mixture; cook and stir about 2 minutes or until sauce thickens. Serve over rice. *Makes 4 servings*

Serving Suggestion: Serve with Egg Drop Soup made by stirring beaten egg into simmering reduced-sodium chicken broth seasoned with chopped fresh herbs, such as cilantro.

stir-fried catfish with cucumber rice

shrimp with snow peas

- **1 pound raw Florida shrimp**
- **½ cup chicken broth**
- **¼ cup soy sauce**
- **3 tablespoons dry sherry or white wine**
- **2 tablespoons cornstarch**
- **2 teaspoons minced fresh ginger**
- **¼ cup vegetable oil**
- **1 (6-ounce) package frozen snow peas, thawed and patted dry,** *or* **½ pound fresh snow peas**
- **3 green onions, cut into 1-inch pieces**
- **½ can (8 ounces) sliced water chestnuts, drained**
- **Hot cooked rice**

Peel shrimp and, if large, cut into halves lengthwise. Combine chicken broth, soy sauce, sherry, cornstarch and ginger in small bowl; set aside. In wok or large skillet, heat oil until hot. Add shrimp. Cook, stirring rapidly, 3 to 4 minutes or until pink; remove. Add snow peas; stir-fry 3 to 4 minutes or until soft. Remove from wok; set aside. Repeat procedure with onions and water chestnuts. Add shrimp, snow peas, onions and water chestnuts to wok. Add chicken broth mixture and cook until sauce thickens slightly, about 2 to 3 minutes. Serve over rice. *Makes 4 servings*

Favorite recipe from **Florida Department of Agriculture and Consumer Services, Bureau of Seafood and Aquaculture**

quick tip

Snow peas are an essential vegetable in Chinese cooking. When purchasing fresh snow peas, look for crisp, brightly colored, flat pods with tiny seeds that are barely visible. To string fresh snow peas, pinch off the tip of the pods at the stem ends and pull away any stringy fibers along the edges. Fresh snow peas will keep for up to three days in the refrigerator.

shrimp with snow peas

beef with leeks and tofu

8 ounces boneless beef top sirloin, top loin (strip) or tenderloin steaks
2 cloves garlic, minced
8 ounces firm tofu, drained
¾ cup chicken broth
¼ cup soy sauce
1 tablespoon dry sherry
1 tablespoon cornstarch
4 teaspoons peanut or vegetable oil, divided
1 large *or* 2 medium leeks, sliced (white and light green portion)
1 large red bell pepper, cut into short, thin strips
1 tablespoon dark sesame oil (optional)
  Hot cooked noodles or spaghetti (optional)

1. Cut beef lengthwise in half, then crosswise into ⅛-inch slices. Toss beef with garlic in medium bowl. Press tofu lightly between paper towels; cut into ¾-inch triangles or squares.

2. Blend broth, soy sauce and sherry into cornstarch in small bowl until smooth.

3. Heat 2 teaspoons peanut oil in wok or large, deep skillet over medium-high heat. Stir-fry beef in batches 2 minutes or until barely pink in center. Remove and set aside.

4. Add remaining 2 teaspoons peanut oil to skillet. Add leek and bell pepper; stir-fry 3 minutes or until bell pepper is crisp-tender. Stir broth mixture; add to wok with tofu. Stir-fry 2 minutes or until sauce boils and thickens and tofu is hot, stirring frequently.

5. Return beef and any accumulated juices to wok; heat through. Stir in sesame oil, if desired. Serve over noodles, if desired.   *Makes 4 servings*

beef with leeks and tofu

chicken and asparagus stir-fry

1 cup uncooked rice
2 tablespoons vegetable oil
1 pound boneless skinless chicken breasts, cut into ½-inch-wide strips
2 medium red bell peppers, cut into thin strips
½ pound fresh asparagus,* cut diagonally into 1-inch pieces
½ cup stir-fry sauce

For stir-frying, select thin stalks of asparagus.

1. Cook rice according to package directions; keep hot.

2. Heat oil in wok or large skillet over medium-high heat. Stir-fry chicken 3 to 4 minutes or until cooked through.

3. Stir in bell peppers and asparagus; reduce heat to medium. Cover; cook 2 minutes or until vegetables are crisp-tender, stirring once or twice.

4. Stir in sauce; heat through. Serve with rice.   *Makes 4 servings*

vegetable-shrimp stir-fry

1 tablespoon olive oil
2 cups snow peas
6 green onions, cut into 1-inch pieces
1 red bell pepper, cut into ½-inch strips
1 pound medium raw shrimp, peeled and deveined
¼ pound large mushrooms, quartered
2 tablespoons soy sauce
1 tablespoon seasoned rice vinegar
1 teaspoon dark sesame oil

1. Heat oil in wok or large skillet over medium-high heat. Add snow peas, green onions and bell pepper; stir-fry 2 minutes.

2. Add shrimp; stir-fry 2 minutes or until shrimp turn pink and opaque. Add mushrooms; stir-fry until most of liquid evaporates.

3. Add soy sauce, vinegar and sesame oil; heat through.
                                              Makes 4 servings

chicken and asparagus stir-fry

mongolian vegetables

1 package (about 12 ounces) firm tofu, drained
4 tablespoons soy sauce, divided
1 tablespoon dark sesame oil
1 large head bok choy (about 1½ pounds)
2 teaspoons cornstarch
1 tablespoon peanut or vegetable oil
1 large red or yellow bell pepper, cut into short, thin strips
2 cloves garlic, minced
4 small *or* 2 large green onions, cut into ½-inch pieces
2 teaspoons toasted sesame seeds*

To toast sesame seeds, spread seeds in small skillet. Shake skillet over medium heat 2 minutes or until seeds begin to pop and turn golden.

1. Press tofu lightly between paper towels; cut into ¾-inch squares or triangles. Place in shallow dish. Combine 2 tablespoons soy sauce and sesame oil; drizzle over tofu. Let stand while preparing vegetables.

2. Cut stems from bok choy leaves; slice stems into ½-inch pieces. Cut leaves crosswise into ½-inch slices.

3. Blend remaining 2 tablespoons soy sauce into cornstarch in small bowl until smooth.

4. Heat peanut oil in wok or large skillet over medium-high heat. Add bok choy stems, bell pepper and garlic; stir-fry 5 minutes. Add onions and bok choy leaves; stir-fry 2 minutes.

5. Stir soy sauce mixture and add to wok along with tofu mixture. Stir-fry 30 seconds or until sauce boils and thickens. Sprinkle with sesame seeds.

Makes 2 main-dish or 4 side-dish servings

mongolian vegetables

five-spice shrimp with walnuts

1 pound medium or large raw shrimp, peeled and deveined
½ teaspoon Chinese five-spice powder*
2 cloves garlic, minced
½ cup chicken broth
2 tablespoons soy sauce
2 tablespoons dry sherry
1 tablespoon cornstarch
1 tablespoon peanut or vegetable oil
1 large red bell pepper, cut into short, thin strips
⅓ cup walnut halves or quarters
   Hot cooked rice
¼ cup thinly sliced green onions (optional)

Chinese five-spice powder is a blend of cinnamon, cloves, fennel seed, anise and Szechuan peppercorns. It is available in most supermarkets and at Asian grocery stores.

1. Toss shrimp with five-spice powder and garlic in small bowl.

2. Blend broth, soy sauce and sherry into cornstarch in cup until smooth.

3. Heat oil in wok or large skillet over medium-high heat. Add shrimp mixture, bell pepper and walnuts; stir-fry 3 to 5 minutes until shrimp are opaque and bell pepper is crisp-tender.

4. Stir broth mixture and add to wok. Stir-fry 1 minute or until sauce boils and thickens. Serve over rice. Garnish with green onions.

Makes 4 servings

quick tip

To devein shrimp, make a small cut along the back and lift out the dark vein with the tip of a knife. You may find the task easier if it is done under cold running water. There are also special gadgets available that make peeling and deveining shrimp a one-step process.

five-spice shrimp with walnuts

main events

sweet and sour chicken

2 tablespoons unseasoned rice vinegar
3 cloves garlic, minced
2 tablespoons soy sauce
½ teaspoon minced fresh ginger
¼ teaspoon red pepper flakes
6 ounces boneless skinless chicken breasts
1 teaspoon vegetable oil
1 large green bell pepper, cut into 1-inch squares
3 green onions, cut into 1-inch pieces
1 tablespoon cornstarch
½ cup reduced-sodium chicken broth
2 tablespoons apricot fruit spread
1 can (11 ounces) mandarin orange segments, drained
2 cups hot cooked rice or Chinese egg noodles

1. Combine vinegar, garlic, soy sauce, ginger and red pepper flakes in medium bowl. Cut chicken into ½-inch strips; toss with vinegar mixture. Marinate 20 minutes at room temperature.

2. Heat oil in wok or large nonstick skillet over medium heat. Drain chicken; reserve marinade. Add chicken to wok; stir-fry 3 minutes. Stir in bell pepper and onions. Stir cornstarch into reserved marinade.

3. Stir broth, fruit spread and marinade mixture into wok. Cook and stir until sauce boils 1 minute and thickens. Add orange segments; heat through. Serve over rice.   *Makes 4 servings*

sweet and sour chicken

szechuan tuna steaks

4 tuna steaks (6 ounces each), cut 1 inch thick
¼ cup dry sherry or sake
¼ cup soy sauce
1 tablespoon dark sesame oil
1 teaspoon hot chili oil *or* **¼ teaspoon red pepper flakes**
1 clove garlic, minced
3 tablespoons chopped fresh cilantro

1. Place tuna in single layer in large shallow glass dish. Combine sherry, soy sauce, sesame oil, hot chili oil and garlic in small bowl. Reserve ¼ cup soy sauce mixture at room temperature. Pour remaining soy sauce mixture over tuna. Cover; marinate in refrigerator 40 minutes, turning once.

2. Spray grid with nonstick cooking spray. Prepare grill for direct grilling.

3. Drain tuna, discarding marinade. Place tuna on grid. Grill, uncovered, over medium-hot coals 6 minutes or until tuna is seared, but still feels somewhat soft in center,* turning halfway through grilling time. Transfer tuna to cutting board. Cut each tuna steak into thin slices; fan out slices onto serving plates. Serve with reserved soy sauce mixture; sprinkle with cilantro.

Makes 4 servings

Tuna becomes dry and tough if overcooked. Cook it to medium doneness for best results.

quick tip

Sesame oil comes in two basic types. Dark sesame oil, which is the kind used in most Asian cuisines, has a strong flavor and fragrance. It is sometimes called toasted sesame oil, or Asian sesame oil. The lighter sesame oil has a much milder flavor and can be used for frying and in salad dressings. Dark sesame oil is a delightful flavor accent, but should be used sparingly as it can easily become overwhelming.

szechuan tuna steak

stir-fried crab

8 ounces firm tofu, drained
1 tablespoon soy sauce
¼ cup chicken broth
3 tablespoons oyster sauce
2 teaspoons cornstarch
1 tablespoon peanut or vegetable oil
2 cups snow peas, cut into halves
8 ounces crabmeat or imitation crabmeat, broken into ½-inch pieces (about 2 cups)
    Sesame Noodle Cake (recipe follows, optional)
2 tablespoons chopped fresh cilantro or thinly sliced green onions

1. Press tofu lightly between paper towels; cut into ½-inch squares or triangles. Place in shallow dish. Drizzle soy sauce over tofu.

2. Blend broth and oyster sauce into cornstarch in small bowl until smooth.

3. Heat oil in wok or large skillet over medium-high heat. Add snow peas; stir-fry 2 to 3 minutes or until crisp-tender. Add crabmeat; stir-fry 1 minute. Stir broth mixture and add to wok. Stir-fry 30 seconds or until sauce boils and thickens.

4. Stir in tofu mixture; heat through. Serve over Sesame Noodle Cake. Sprinkle with cilantro.   *Makes 4 servings*

sesame noodle cake

4 ounces uncooked thin Chinese egg noodles or vermicelli
1 tablespoon soy sauce
1 tablespoon peanut or vegetable oil
½ teaspoon dark sesame oil

1. Cook noodles according to package directions; drain well. Place in large bowl. Toss with soy sauce until sauce is absorbed.

continued on page 50

stir-fried crab

sesame noodle cake, continued

2. Heat peanut oil in large nonstick skillet over medium heat. Add noodle mixture; pat into even layer with spatula.

3. Cook, uncovered, 6 minutes or until bottom is lightly browned. Invert onto plate, then slide back into skillet, browned side up. Cook 4 minutes or until bottom is well browned. Drizzle with sesame oil. Transfer to serving platter and cut into quarters. *Makes 4 servings*

orange beef

1 pound boneless beef top sirloin or tenderloin steaks
2 cloves garlic, minced
1 teaspoon grated fresh orange peel
2 tablespoons soy sauce
2 tablespoons orange juice
1 tablespoon dry sherry
1 tablespoon cornstarch
1 tablespoon peanut or vegetable oil
   Hot cooked rice
   Orange peel strips or orange slices (optional)

1. Cut beef in half lengthwise, then crosswise into thin slices. Toss with garlic and orange peel in medium bowl.

2. Blend soy sauce, orange juice and sherry into cornstarch in small bowl until smooth.

3. Heat oil in wok or large skillet over medium-high heat. Stir-fry beef in batches 2 to 3 minutes or until barely pink in center. Stir soy sauce mixture and add to wok. Stir-fry 30 seconds or until sauce boils and thickens. Serve over rice; garnish with orange peel strips. *Makes 4 servings*

orange beef

cellophane noodles with pork

1 package (about 4 ounces) cellophane noodles*
32 dried shiitake mushrooms
2 tablespoons minced fresh ginger
2 tablespoons black bean sauce
1½ cups chicken broth
1 tablespoon dry sherry
1 tablespoon soy sauce
2 tablespoons vegetable oil
6 ounces lean ground pork
1 small jalapeño or other hot pepper,** seeded and finely chopped
3 green onions, sliced
    Cilantro and fresh hot red peppers (optional)

Cellophane noodles (also called bean threads or glass noodles) are clear, thin noodles sold in tangled bunches.

**Jalapeño peppers can sting and irritate the skin, so wear rubber gloves when handling peppers and do not touch your eyes.*

1. Place noodles and dried mushrooms in separate bowls; cover each with hot water. Let stand 30 minutes; drain. Cut noodles into 4-inch pieces.

2. Squeeze out excess water from mushrooms. Cut off and discard mushroom stems; cut caps into thin slices.

3. Combine ginger and black bean sauce in small bowl. Combine broth, sherry and soy sauce in another small bowl; set aside.

4. Heat oil in wok or large skillet over high heat. Add pork; stir-fry about 2 minutes or until no longer pink. Add jalapeño, green onions and black bean sauce mixture. Stir-fry 1 minute.

5. Add broth mixture, noodles and mushrooms. Simmer, uncovered, until most of the liquid is absorbed, about 5 minutes. Garnish with cilantro and red peppers. *Makes 4 servings*

cellophane noodles with pork

moo shu beef

½ **pound deli roast beef, sliced ⅛ inch thick**
1 **tablespoon dry sherry**
3 **teaspoons soy sauce, divided**
2 **teaspoons cornstarch, divided**
1 **teaspoon minced fresh ginger**
1 **clove garlic, minced**
½ **teaspoon sugar**
¼ **cup cold water**
¼ **cup beef broth**
3 **tablespoons peanut or vegetable oil, divided**
1 **egg, lightly beaten**
1 **cup shredded carrots**
1 **can (8 ounces) sliced bamboo shoots, drained and cut into thin strips**
3 **green onions, cut into ½-inch pieces**
   Hoisin* or plum sauce
8 **flour tortillas (7 to 8 inches), warmed**

*Hoisin sauce is a thick, dark brown sauce made from soybeans, sugar, spices, garlic, chili peppers and salt. It has a sweet, spicy flavor.

1. Cut beef into thin strips. Combine sherry, 1 teaspoon soy sauce, 1 teaspoon cornstarch, ginger, garlic and sugar in large bowl; stir until smooth. Add beef and toss to coat. Marinate 10 minutes.

2. Stir water, broth and remaining 2 teaspoons soy sauce into remaining 1 teaspoon cornstarch in small bowl until smooth; set aside.

3. Heat wok or large skillet over high heat about 1 minute or until hot. Drizzle 1 tablespoon oil into wok and heat 30 seconds. Pour egg into wok; tilt to coat bottom. Scramble egg, breaking into small pieces as it cooks. Remove from wok.

4. Add remaining 2 tablespoons oil to wok and heat 30 seconds. Add carrots; stir-fry 1 minute. Add beef mixture, bamboo shoots and green onions; stir-fry 1 minute. Stir broth mixture; add to wok. Cook and stir 1 minute or until sauce boils and thickens. Cook 1 minute more. Stir in egg.

5. Spread hoisin sauce on each tortilla. Spoon beef mixture over sauce. Fold tortillas over filling.   *Makes 4 servings*

scallops with vegetables

1 package (1 ounce) dried shiitake mushrooms
4 teaspoons cornstarch
1 cup cold water
2½ tablespoons dry sherry
4 teaspoons soy sauce
2 teaspoons chicken bouillon granules
2 tablespoons vegetable oil
8 ounces green beans, cut into 1-inch pieces
2 yellow onions, cut into wedges
3 stalks celery, cut into ½-inch pieces
2 teaspoons minced fresh ginger
1 clove garlic, minced
1 pound sea scallops, cut into quarters
6 green onions, sliced
1 can (15 ounces) baby corn, drained

1. Place mushrooms in bowl; cover with hot water. Let stand 30 minutes; drain. Squeeze out as much water as possible from mushrooms. Remove and discard stems; cut caps into thin slices.

2. Blend cornstarch and cold water in small bowl; stir in sherry, soy sauce and bouillon granules. Set aside.

3. Heat oil in wok or large skillet over high heat. Add green beans, yellow onions, celery, ginger and garlic; stir-fry 3 minutes.

4. Stir cornstarch mixture; add to wok. Cook and stir until sauce boils and thickens.

5. Add mushrooms, scallops, green onions and baby corn. Stir-fry until scallops turn opaque, about 4 minutes.   *Makes 4 to 6 servings*

beef and asparagus stir-fry

¾ cup water
3 tablespoons soy sauce
3 tablespoons hoisin sauce
1 tablespoon cornstarch
1 tablespoon peanut or vegetable oil
1 pound sirloin steak, cut into thin strips
1 teaspoon dark sesame oil
8 shiitake mushrooms, stems removed and thinly sliced
1 cup baby corn
8 ounces asparagus (8 to 10 medium spears), cut into 1-inch pieces
1 cup sugar snap peas or snow peas
½ cup red bell pepper strips
½ cup cherry tomato halves (optional)

1. Whisk water, soy sauce and hoisin sauce into cornstarch in small bowl; set aside.

2. Heat peanut oil in wok or large skillet over medium-high heat. Add beef; stir-fry 5 to 6 minutes or until still slightly pink. Remove beef to plate with slotted spoon.

3. Add sesame oil, mushrooms and baby corn to skillet; stir-fry 2 to 3 minutes or until mushrooms are tender and corn is heated through. Add asparagus, sugar snap peas and bell peppers; cook and stir 1 minute or until crisp-tender.

4. Return beef with any juices to skillet. Stir soy sauce mixture and add to wok; add tomatoes, if desired. Cook and stir 1 minute or until heated through and sauce thickens. *Makes 4 servings*

beef and asparagus stir-fry

grilled chinese salmon

3 tablespoons soy sauce
2 tablespoons dry sherry
2 cloves garlic, minced
1 pound salmon fillets or steaks
2 tablespoons finely chopped fresh cilantro

1. Combine soy sauce, sherry and garlic in shallow dish. Add salmon; turn to coat. Cover; refrigerate at least 30 minutes or up to 2 hours.

2. Prepare grill for direct cooking or preheat broiler. Remove salmon from dish; reserve marinade. Arrange fillets skin side down on oiled grid over hot coals or on oiled broiler pan. Broil or grill 10 minutes or until fish begins to flake when tested with fork. Baste with reserved marinade after 5 minutes of cooking; discard any remaining marinade. Sprinkle with cilantro.

Makes 4 servings

szechuan pork and vegetables

4 butterflied pork loin chops, ½ inch thick (1 to 1¼ pounds)
¼ cup plus 1 tablespoon stir-fry sauce, divided
½ teaspoon minced fresh ginger
1 package (16 ounces) frozen Asian-style vegetables, thawed
1 can (5 ounces) crisp chow mein noodles
2 tablespoons chopped green onion

1. Heat large, deep nonstick skillet over medium heat; add pork. Spoon 1 tablespoon stir-fry sauce over pork; sprinkle with ginger. Cook 3 minutes. Turn pork; cook 3 minutes. Transfer to plate; set aside.

2. Add vegetables and remaining ¼ cup stir-fry sauce to skillet. Cook over medium-low heat 3 minutes; add pork. Cook 3 minutes or until pork is barely pink in center, stirring vegetables and turning chops once.

3. Arrange chow mein noodles on 4 serving plates. Top with vegetable mixture and pork; sprinkle with green onion.

Makes 4 servings

Prep and Cook Time: 12 minutes

grilled chinese salmon

mongolian hot pot

2 ounces cellophane noodles (bean threads)
½ pound boneless beef top sirloin or tenderloin steaks
1 can (about 48 ounces) chicken broth
½ pound pork tenderloin, cut into ⅛-inch slices
½ pound medium raw shrimp, peeled and deveined
½ pound sea scallops, cut lengthwise into halves
½ pound small fresh mushrooms
Dipping Sauce (recipe follows)
1 pound spinach

1. Place noodles in medium bowl; cover with warm water. Soak until soft and pliable. Drain well and cut into 2-inch lengths; set aside.

2. Cut beef lengthwise in half, then crosswise into ⅛-inch slices.

3. Heat broth in electric skillet to a simmer (or, bring half of broth to a simmer in fondue pot, keeping remaining broth hot for replacement).

4. Arrange beef, pork, shrimp, scallops and mushrooms on large platter.

5. Prepare Dipping Sauce.

6. To serve, select food from platter and cook it in simmering broth until cooked through, using chop sticks or long-handled fork. Serve with Dipping Sauce.

7. After all food is cooked, stir spinach into broth and heat until wilted. (Cook spinach in two batches if using fondue pot.) Place noodles in individual soup bowls. Ladle broth mixture into bowls. Season with Dipping Sauce, if desired.   *Makes 4 to 6 servings*

Dipping Sauce: Combine ½ cup soy sauce, ¼ cup dry sherry and 1 tablespoon dark sesame oil in small bowl; transfer to individual dipping bowls.

mongolian hot pot

chinese pork & vegetable stir-fry

2 tablespoons BERTOLLI® Olive Oil, divided
1 pound pork tenderloin or boneless beef sirloin, cut into ¼-inch slices
6 cups assorted fresh vegetables*
1 can (8 ounces) sliced water chestnuts, drained
1 envelope LIPTON® RECIPE SECRETS® Onion Soup Mix
¾ cup water
½ cup orange juice
1 tablespoon soy sauce
¼ teaspoon garlic powder

*Use any combination of the following: broccoli florets; thinly sliced red or green bell peppers; snow peas or thinly sliced carrots.

1. In 12-inch skillet, heat 1 tablespoon olive oil over medium-high heat; brown pork. Remove and set aside.

2. In same skillet, heat remaining 1 tablespoon olive oil and cook assorted fresh vegetables, stirring occasionally, 5 minutes. Stir in water chestnuts, soup mix blended with water, orange juice, soy sauce and garlic powder. Bring to a boil over high heat. Reduce heat to low and simmer uncovered, 3 minutes. Return pork to skillet and cook 1 minute or until heated through.

Makes about 4 servings

Tip: Pick up pre-sliced vegetables from your local salad bar.

chinese pork & vegetable stir-fry

shrimp in mock lobster sauce

½ cup reduced-sodium beef or chicken broth
¼ cup oyster sauce
1 tablespoon cornstarch
1 egg
1 egg white
1 tablespoon peanut or canola oil
¾ pound medium or large raw shrimp, peeled and deveined
2 cloves garlic, minced
3 green onions, cut into ½-inch pieces
Hot cooked Chinese egg noodles

1. Stir broth and oyster sauce into cornstarch in small bowl until smooth. Beat egg with egg white in separate small bowl; set aside.

2. Heat wok or large skillet over medium-high heat 1 minute or until hot. Drizzle oil into wok and heat 30 seconds. Add shrimp and garlic; stir-fry 3 to 5 minutes or until shrimp turn pink and opaque.

3. Stir broth mixture; add to wok. Add onions; stir-fry 1 minute or until sauce boils and thickens.

4. Stir eggs into wok; stir-fry 1 minute or just until eggs are set. Serve over noodles.   *Makes 4 servings*

quick tip

Oyster sauce is a rich-tasting, dark brown sauce made from oysters, soy sauce and, often, MSG. Check the label to see if the sauce you're purchasing contains real oyster extract or just oyster flavoring. After opening, store oyster sauce in the refrigerator.

shrimp in mock lobster sauce

quick chicken

chicken with lychees

¼ cup plus 1 teaspoon cornstarch, divided

3 boneless skinless chicken breasts (about 1 pound), cut into bite-size pieces

½ cup water, divided

½ cup tomato sauce

1 teaspoon sugar

1 teaspoon chicken bouillon granules

3 tablespoons vegetable oil

6 green onions with tops, cut into 1-inch pieces

1 red bell pepper, cut into 1-inch pieces

1 can (about 11 ounces) whole peeled lychees, drained

Hot cooked cellophane noodles

1. Place ¼ cup cornstarch in large resealable food storage bag; add chicken. Seal bag; shake until chicken is well coated.

2. Blend ¼ cup water into remaining 1 teaspoon cornstarch in small bowl; mix well. Combine remaining ¼ cup water, tomato sauce, sugar and bouillon granules in small bowl; mix well.

3. Heat oil in wok or large skillet over high heat. Add chicken; stir-fry 5 to 8 minutes or until lightly browned. Add onions and bell pepper; stir-fry 1 minute. Pour tomato sauce mixture over chicken mixture. Stir in lychees. Reduce heat to low; cover. Simmer about 5 minutes or until chicken is cooked through.

4. Stir cornstarch mixture; add to wok. Cook and stir until sauce boils and thickens. Serve over hot cellophane noodles. *Makes 4 servings*

chicken with lychees

golden chicken stir-fry

½ **pound chicken tenders, cut into thin strips**
½ **cup stir-fry sauce, divided**
 3 **tablespoons vegetable oil, divided**
 1 **medium onion, thinly sliced**
 2 **carrots, cut diagonally into thin slices**
 1 **stalk celery, cut diagonally into thin slices**
 1 **clove garlic, minced**
 1 **tablespoon sesame seeds, toasted**
½ **teaspoon Chinese five-spice powder**
¼ **teaspoon dark sesame oil**
   Hot cooked rice

1. Toss chicken with 2 tablespoons stir-fry sauce in small bowl. Heat
1 tablespoon vegetable oil in wok or large skillet over medium-high heat.
Add chicken and stir-fry 2 minutes; remove and set aside.

2. Heat remaining 2 tablespoons vegetable oil in wok. Add onion; stir-fry
2 minutes. Add carrots, celery and garlic; stir-fry 2 minutes.

3. Add remaining stir-fry sauce, chicken mixture, sesame seeds and five-spice
powder. Cook and stir until chicken and vegetables are coated with sauce.
Remove from heat; stir in sesame oil. Serve with rice.   *Makes 4 servings*

quick tip

*There are two secrets to cooking perfect rice—use very low heat and don't
open the pot until 20 minutes are up. Opening the pot before the rice is done
lets heat and moisture escape and can make a big difference in the finished
rice. If you don't have a burner that holds a low simmer, invest in a device
called a "heat diffuser" or "flame tamer". This round, inexpensive, perforated
disk can be purchased in cookware and hardware stores.*

golden chicken stir-fry

chicken with snow peas

1½ pounds boneless skinless chicken breasts, cut into bite-size pieces
6 tablespoons soy sauce, divided
¼ cup all-purpose flour
2 tablespoons sugar
½ teaspoon ground ginger
1 clove garlic, minced
2 tablespoons vegetable oil
4 ounces shiitake or other fresh wild mushrooms, stemmed and cut into long thin strips
1 red bell pepper, cut into bite-size pieces
1½ cups (4 ounces) snow peas, trimmed
1½ cups chicken broth
1 tablespoon cornstarch
¼ teaspoon black pepper
Hot cooked rice

1. Combine chicken and 3 tablespoons soy sauce in medium bowl. Cover and refrigerate 15 minutes to 1 hour.

2. Combine flour, sugar, ginger and garlic in pie plate. Drain chicken, discarding marinade. Roll chicken in flour mixture.

3. Heat oil in wok or large skillet over high heat. Add chicken; stir-fry 3 to 4 minutes or until no longer pink.

4. Add mushrooms; stir-fry 1 minute. Add bell pepper and snow peas; stir-fry 1 to 2 minutes or until crisp-tender.

5. Whisk together remaining 3 tablespoons soy sauce, chicken broth, cornstarch and black pepper in small bowl; add to chicken mixture in wok. Cook and stir until sauce boils and thickens. Serve with rice.

Makes 5 to 6 servings

chicken with snow peas

pineapple teriyaki chicken

½ small red onion, halved and thinly sliced
1 medium green and/or red bell pepper, cut into 1-inch pieces
6 boneless, skinless chicken breasts (about 1½ pounds)
1 can (20 ounces) pineapple rings, drained
1 cup LAWRY'S® Teriyaki Marinade, divided

Preheat oven to 375°F. Spray 13×9×2-inch glass baking dish with nonstick cooking spray; add onion and bell pepper. Arrange chicken over vegetables. Top with pineapple, then drizzle with Marinade. Bake 40 minutes, or until chicken is thoroughly cooked. Spoon pan juices over chicken and vegetables once during baking and again just before serving.   *Makes 6 servings*

Meal Idea: Great served over cooked white rice.

Prep. Time: 10 minutes
Cook Time: 45 minutes

mandarin orange chicken

2 tablespoons rice vinegar
2 tablespoons olive oil, divided
2 tablespoons soy sauce
2 teaspoons grated orange peel
1 clove garlic, minced
1 pound boneless skinless chicken breasts, cut into strips
2 cans (11 ounces each) mandarin oranges, undrained
½ cup orange juice
2 tablespoons cornstarch
½ teaspoon red pepper flakes
1 onion, cut into thin wedges
1 small zucchini, sliced
1 red bell pepper, cut into bite-size pieces
1 can (3 ounces) chow mein noodles (optional)

continued on page 74

pineapple teriyaki chicken

mandarin orange chicken, continued

1. Combine vinegar, 1 tablespoon oil, soy sauce, orange peel and garlic in medium bowl. Add chicken; toss to coat well. Cover and refrigerate 15 minutes to 1 hour.

2. Drain chicken, reserving marinade. Drain oranges into 2-cup measuring cup; set oranges aside. Add enough orange juice to make 2 cups liquid. Stir orange juice mixture into cornstarch and red pepper flakes in medium bowl.

3. Heat remaining 1 tablespoon oil in wok or large skillet over high heat. Add chicken; stir-fry 2 to 3 minutes or until cooked through. Remove chicken.

4. Stir-fry onion 1 minute over high heat. Add zucchini; stir-fry 1 minute. Add bell pepper; stir-fry 1 minute or until all vegetables are crisp-tender. Stir in orange juice mixture. Cook and stir until mixture comes to a boil; boil 1 minute. Add chicken, cook until hot. Gently stir in oranges.

Makes 6 servings

chicken wraps

½ **pound boneless skinless chicken thighs**
½ **teaspoon Chinese five-spice powder**
½ **cup bean sprouts**
2 **tablespoons minced green onion**
2 **tablespoons sliced almonds**
2 **tablespoons soy sauce**
4 **teaspoons hoisin sauce**
1 to 2 **teaspoons chili garlic sauce**
4 **large romaine, iceberg or bibb lettuce leaves**

1. Preheat oven to 350°F. Place chicken thighs on baking sheet; sprinkle with five-spice powder. Bake 20 minutes or until chicken is cooked through. Cool.

2. Dice chicken. Combine chicken, bean sprouts, green onion, almonds, soy sauce, hoisin sauce and chili garlic sauce in large bowl. To serve, spoon ⅓ cup chicken mixture onto each lettuce leaf.

Makes 4 servings

chicken wrap

gingered chicken with vegetables

2 tablespoons vegetable oil, divided
1 pound boneless skinless chicken breasts, cut into thin strips
1 cup red pepper strips
1 cup sliced fresh mushrooms
16 fresh pea pods, cut in half crosswise
½ cup sliced water chestnuts
¼ cup sliced green onions
1 tablespoon grated fresh gingerroot
1 large clove garlic, crushed
⅔ cup reduced-fat, reduced-sodium chicken broth
2 tablespoons EQUAL® SPOONFUL*
2 tablespoons light soy sauce
4 teaspoons cornstarch
2 teaspoons dark sesame oil
    Salt and pepper to taste

*May substitute 3 packets EQUAL® sweetener.

● Heat 1 tablespoon vegetable oil in large skillet over medium-high heat. Stir-fry chicken until no longer pink; remove chicken from skillet. Heat remaining 1 tablespoon vegetable oil in skillet. Add bell peppers, mushrooms, pea pods, water chestnuts, green onions, ginger and garlic to skillet. Stir-fry mixture 3 to 4 minutes until vegetables are crisp-tender.

● Meanwhile, combine chicken broth, Equal®, soy sauce, cornstarch and sesame oil until smooth. Stir into skillet mixture. Cook over medium heat until thick and clear. Stir in chicken; heat through. Season with salt and pepper to taste.

● Serve over hot cooked rice, if desired.   *Makes 4 servings*

gingered chicken with vegetables

cashew chicken

10 ounces boneless skinless chicken breasts, cut into bite-size pieces
1 tablespoon dry white wine
1 tablespoon soy sauce
1 tablespoon cornstarch
½ teaspoon garlic powder
1 teaspoon vegetable oil
6 green onions, cut into 1-inch pieces
2 cups sliced mushrooms
1 red or green bell pepper, cut into strips
1 can (6 ounces) sliced water chestnuts, rinsed and drained
2 tablespoons hoisin sauce (optional)
   Hot cooked rice
¼ cup cashews, toasted

1. Place chicken in large resealable food storage bag. Stir wine and soy sauce into cornstarch and garlic powder in small bowl until smooth. Pour over chicken pieces. Seal bag; turn to coat. Marinate in refrigerator 1 hour. Drain chicken; discard marinade.

2. Heat oil in wok or large nonstick skillet over medium-high heat. Add onions; stir-fry 1 minute. Add chicken; stir-fry 2 minutes or until browned. Add mushrooms, bell pepper and water chestnuts; stir-fry 3 minutes or until vegetables are crisp-tender and chicken is cooked through. Stir in hoisin sauce; cook and stir 1 minute or until heated through.

3. Serve chicken and vegetables over rice with cashews.

Makes 4 servings

quick tip

Did you ever wonder why cashews are always sold without their shells? The reason is that there is a highly toxic liquid within the shell that must be removed during processing. Cashews have a sweet, buttery flavor because of their high concentration of fat. For this reason, they should be stored refrigerated or frozen to prevent rancidity.

cashew chicken

honey-glazed chicken

1 can (20 ounces) pineapple chunks in juice
1 tablespoon cornstarch
2 tablespoons honey
1 tablespoon Dijon mustard
½ teaspoon ground ginger
¼ teaspoon red pepper flakes
1 tablespoon oil
1 pound boneless skinless chicken breasts, cut into 2-inch pieces
1 green or red bell pepper, cut into pieces
Hot cooked rice (optional)

1. Drain pineapple into small bowl; reserve pineapple. Stir cornstarch into juice in small bowl until smooth. Add honey, mustard, ginger and red pepper flakes; mix well.

2. Heat oil in wok or large skillet over medium-high heat. Add chicken; stir-fry 5 minutes or until browned. Add bell pepper; stir-fry 3 minutes. Add reserved pineapple and juice mixture. Bring to a boil. Reduce heat to medium-low. Simmer 5 to 8 minutes or until chicken is cooked through and sauce thickens. Serve with rice. *Makes 4 servings*

Prep Time: 5 minutes
Cook Time: 10 minutes

quick tip

It's usually a good idea to make more rice than you will need at one meal when you're preparing it. Extra rice can be refrigerated for several days and used in other recipes. In fact, rice that has been refrigerated works much better than freshly cooked in fried rice recipes because it clumps together less. Rice can also be frozen for up to 3 months. Reheat by steaming over hot water or defrosting in the microwave.

honey-glazed chicken

chicken with walnuts

1 cup uncooked instant rice
½ cup chicken broth
¼ cup Chinese plum sauce
2 tablespoons soy sauce
2 teaspoons cornstarch
2 tablespoons vegetable oil, divided
1 bag (3 cups) frozen bell pepper and onion mix, thawed
1 pound boneless skinless chicken breasts, cut into ¼-inch strips
1 clove garlic, minced
1 cup walnut halves

1. Cook rice according to package directions. Set aside and keep warm.

2. Stir broth, plum sauce and soy sauce into cornstarch in medium bowl; set aside.

3. Heat 1 tablespoon oil in wok or large skillet over medium-high heat. Add peppers and onions; stir-fry 3 minutes or until crisp-tender. Remove vegetables from wok. Drain and discard liquid.

4. Heat remaining 1 tablespoon oil in same wok. Add chicken and garlic; stir-fry 3 minutes or until chicken is cooked through.

5. Stir broth mixture; add to wok. Cook and stir 1 minute or until sauce comes to a boil and thickens. Stir in vegetables and walnuts; cook 1 minute more. Serve over rice. *Makes 4 servings*

Prep and Cook Time: 20 minutes

chicken with walnuts

chicken stir-fry

4 boneless skinless chicken breast halves (about 1½ pounds)
2 tablespoons vegetable oil
2 tablespoons orange juice
2 tablespoons light soy sauce
1 tablespoon cornstarch
1 bag (16 ounces) BIRDS EYE® frozen Farm Fresh Mixtures Broccoli, Carrots & Water Chestnuts

- Cut chicken into ½-inch-thick long strips.

- In wok or large skillet, heat oil over medium-high heat.

- Add chicken; cook 5 minutes, stirring occasionally.

- Meanwhile, in small bowl, combine orange juice, soy sauce and cornstarch; blend well and set aside.

- Add vegetables to chicken; cook 5 minutes more or until chicken is no longer pink in center, stirring occasionally.

- Stir in soy sauce mixture; cook 1 minute or until heated through.

Makes 4 servings

Serving Suggestion: Serve over hot cooked rice.

Birds Eye Idea: When cooking rice, add one teaspoon lemon juice to each quart of water you use so the grains will stay white and separate.

Prep Time: 5 minutes
Cook Time: 12 minutes

chicken stir-fry

noodles & rice

chicken chow mein

2 teaspoons vegetable oil, divided
1 pound boneless skinless chicken breasts, cut into thin strips
2 cloves garlic, minced
2 tablespoons dry sherry
2 tablespoons soy sauce
2 cups (6 ounces) fresh snow peas, cut into halves
3 green onions, cut diagonally into 1-inch pieces
4 ounces uncooked Chinese egg noodles or vermicelli, cooked and
drained
1 teaspoon dark sesame oil (optional)

1. Heat 1 teaspoon vegetable oil in wok or large nonstick skillet over medium-high heat. Add chicken and garlic; stir-fry 3 minutes or until chicken is no longer pink. Transfer to medium bowl; toss with sherry and soy sauce.

2. Heat remaining 1 teaspoon vegetable oil in wok. Add snow peas; stir-fry 1 minute. Add green onions; stir-fry 30 seconds. Add chicken mixture; stir-fry 1 minute.

3. Add noodles to wok; stir-fry 2 minutes or until heated through. Stir in sesame oil, if desired. *Makes 4 servings*

chicken chow mein

chinese noodles and soy beef

1 boneless beef top sirloin steak (about ¾ pound), cut into thin strips
¼ cup reduced-sodium soy sauce, divided
1 cup water
1 tablespoon cornstarch
1 tablespoon packed brown sugar
1 teaspoon beef bouillon granules
½ teaspoon Chinese five-spice powder (optional)
⅛ teaspoon red pepper flakes
4 ounces uncooked thin noodles or spaghetti
   Nonstick cooking spray
2 cloves garlic, minced
1 teaspoon grated fresh ginger
1 cup thinly sliced onions
½ red bell pepper, thinly sliced
1 cup snow peas
1 can (8 ounces) bamboo shoots, well drained

1. Combine beef strips and 2 tablespoons soy sauce in large resealable food storage bag. Seal bag; turn to coat. Marinate 15 minutes, turning occasionally.

2. Blend water, cornstarch, brown sugar, bouillon granules, five-spice powder and red pepper flakes in medium bowl. Stir until completely dissolved; set aside.

3. Cook noodles according to package directions. Drain; set aside.

4. Spray wok or large nonstick skillet with cooking spray; heat over high heat. Add beef, garlic and ginger to wok; cook, stirring constantly, 3 minutes or until liquid evaporates. Remove and set aside. Reduce heat to medium-high. Add onions and bell pepper; cook, stirring constantly, 3 to 4 minutes or until crisp-tender.

5. Stir reserved cornstarch mixture. Add snow peas, bamboo shoots, cornstarch mixture and beef to skillet; cook 1 to 2 minutes or until sauce boils and thickens. Gently stir in cooked noodles and remaining 2 tablespoons soy sauce. *Makes 4 servings*

chinese noodles and soy beef

fried noodle and pork stir-fry

Noodle Bundles (recipe follows)
½ **cup stir-fry sauce**
¼ **cup red wine**
 1 **teaspoon hot pepper sauce**
½ **teaspoon cornstarch**
 2 **tablespoons peanut oil, divided**
¾ **pound boneless pork tenderloin, cut into thin pieces**
 1 **carrot, thinly sliced**
 1 **medium onion, chopped**
 2 **stalks celery, thinly sliced**
 1 **medium red bell pepper, cut into thin strips**

1. Prepare Noodle Bundles; set aside and keep warm.

2. Blend stir-fry sauce, wine and hot pepper sauce into cornstarch in small bowl; set aside.

3. Heat 1 tablespoon oil in wok or large skillet over high heat. Add pork; stir-fry 3 minutes and remove from wok. Add remaining 1 tablespoon oil and carrot to wok; stir-fry 1 minute. Add onion, celery and bell pepper; stir-fry 3 minutes or until vegetables are tender.

4. Return pork to wok; stir sauce mixture and add to wok. Cook and stir until sauce thickens. Serve over noodle bundles.   *Makes 4 to 6 servings*

Noodle Bundles: Cook 8 ounces thin noodles according to package directions; rinse and drain. Arrange noodles into 4 to 6 bundles. Heat 1 tablespoon peanut oil in large nonstick skillet over medium-high heat. Add 2 to 3 bundles to skillet; cook 5 minutes or until bottoms of bundles are golden. Repeat with remaining bundles, adding more oil to pan as needed.

fried noodle and pork stir-fry

pineapple ham fried rice

8 ounces cooked ham steak, cut ½ inch thick

3 tablespoons vegetable oil, divided

2 tablespoons sliced almonds

1 small green bell pepper, cut into strips

2 green onions with tops, coarsely chopped

4 cups cooked rice, cooled

1 can (8 ounces) pineapple chunks in juice, undrained

2 tablespoons dark raisins

2 to 3 tablespoons reduced-sodium soy sauce

1 tablespoon dark sesame oil

1. Cut ham into 2-inch strips; set aside.

2. Heat wok or large skillet over medium-high heat 1 minute. Drizzle 1 tablespoon vegetable oil into wok and heat 30 seconds. Add almonds; stir-fry until golden brown. Remove from wok.

3. Add remaining 2 tablespoons vegetable oil to wok and heat 30 seconds. Add ham, bell pepper and onions; stir-fry 2 minutes. Add rice, pineapple with juice and raisins; stir-fry until heated through.

4. Stir in soy sauce and sesame oil; stir-fry until well mixed. Transfer to serving bowl. Sprinkle with almonds just before serving.

Makes 4 to 6 servings

quick tip

To make perfect fried rice it's best to start out with cold, leftover rice from the refrigerator. If rice is warm and freshly prepared it can turn to mush when you try to stir-fry it. Cold rice is firmer and less moist. If you do choose to use freshly cooked rice, let it cool, uncovered, before starting. Since fried rice was invented to use up leftovers, feel free to add your own twists to the recipe. Most leftover meat and vegetables work as long as they are not in sauce or gravy. (Excess moisture turns fried rice into fried mush.)

pineapple ham fried rice

crispy orange vegetables and tofu

6 ounces thin noodles or spaghetti
8 ounces firm tofu, drained and cut into 1-inch cubes
1 tablespoon soy sauce
1½ cups vegetable broth or water
2 tablespoons cornstarch
1 tablespoon vegetable oil
2 cups sliced celery
1 cup broccoli florets
¾ cup red bell pepper chunks
⅓ cup sliced green onions
8 strips orange peel
1 teaspoon minced fresh ginger
Orange slices (optional)

1. Cook noodles according to package directions; drain and keep warm. Meanwhile, combine tofu and soy sauce in medium bowl; set aside. Stir vegetable broth into cornstarch in small bowl until smooth.

2. Heat oil in wok or large nonstick skillet. Add celery, broccoli, bell pepper, green onions, orange peel and ginger. Stir-fry about 4 to 5 minutes or until vegetables are crisp-tender. Stir cornstarch mixture and add to vegetable mixture; bring to a boil, stirring constantly until sauce thickens.

3. Gently stir in tofu mixture; cook about 1 minute or until heated through. Serve over noodles. Garnish with orange slices.   *Makes 4 servings*

crispy orange vegetables and tofu

cellophane noodle salad

1 package (about 4 ounces) cellophane noodles
2 tablespoons peanut or vegetable oil
8 ounces medium or large raw shrimp, peeled and deveined
3 cloves garlic, minced
¼ teaspoon red pepper flakes
½ cup cooked pork or ham strips (optional)
2 tablespoons soy sauce
1 tablespoon fresh lemon juice
1 tablespoon unseasoned rice vinegar
1 tablespoon dark sesame oil
⅓ cup thinly sliced green onions or coarsely chopped fresh cilantro

1. Place cellophane noodles in medium bowl; cover with warm water. Soak 15 minutes to soften. Drain well; cut into 2-inch pieces.

2. Meanwhile, heat wok or large skillet over medium-high heat. Add peanut oil; heat until hot. Add shrimp, garlic and red pepper flakes; stir-fry 2 minutes. Add pork, if desired, soy sauce, lemon juice, vinegar and sesame oil; stir-fry 1 minute.

3. Add cellophane noodles; stir-fry 1 minute or until heated through. Serve warm, chilled or at room temperature. Sprinkle with green onions before serving. *Makes 4 servings*

quick tip

Cellophane noodles are also called glass noodles, bean thread noodles and Chinese vermicelli. They are translucent noodles made from mung bean starch and sold in tangled bundles. Cellophane noodles need to be soaked briefly to soften before use in a stir-fry. They can be added without soaking to soups. Another use is to deep fry cellophane noodles for a few seconds. This turns them crisp and opaque.

cellophane noodle salad

asian beef and orange packets

1 beef flank steak (about 1 pound)

2 cups uncooked instant rice

4 sheets (18×12 inches) heavy-duty foil, sprayed lightly with nonstick cooking spray

½ teaspoon black pepper

1 green bell pepper, cut into thin strips

1 red bell pepper, cut into thin strips

½ cup teriyaki sauce

¼ cup orange marmalade

1 can (11 ounces) mandarin orange segments, drained

8 ice cubes

1 cup beef broth or water

1 green onion, sliced (optional)

1. Preheat oven to 450°F.

2. Cut flank steak lengthwise in half, then crosswise into thin slices. Place ½ cup rice in center of each sheet of foil. Divide beef strips into 4 equal portions and arrange to cover rice in each packet. Sprinkle each packet with ⅛ teaspoon black pepper.

3. Arrange one fourth of bell pepper strips on beef. Combine teriyaki sauce and marmalade in small bowl. Spoon teriyaki sauce mixture evenly onto each packet.

4. Arrange one fourth of orange segments around beef and rice in each packet. Place 2 ice cubes on top. Fold up sides of foil and pour ¼ cup broth into each packet.

5. Double fold sides and ends of foil to seal packet, leaving head space for heat circulation. Place packets on baking sheet.

6. Bake 20 minutes or until beef and vegetables are tender. Remove from oven. Let stand 5 minutes. Open packets and transfer contents to serving plates. Garnish with green onion, if desired.   *Makes 4 servings*

asian beef and orange packet

szechuan vegetable lo mein

2 cans (about 14 ounces each) vegetable or chicken broth

2 teaspoons minced garlic

1 teaspoon minced fresh ginger

¼ teaspoon red pepper flakes

1 package (16 ounces) frozen vegetable medley, such as broccoli, carrots, water chestnuts and red bell peppers

1 package (5 ounces) Asian curly noodles or 5 ounces angel hair pasta, broken in half

3 tablespoons soy sauce

1 tablespoon dark sesame oil

¼ cup thinly sliced green onion tops

1. Combine broth, garlic, ginger and red pepper flakes in large deep skillet. Cover and bring to a boil over high heat.

2. Add vegetables and noodles to skillet; cover and return to a boil. Reduce heat to medium-low; simmer, uncovered, 5 to 6 minutes or until noodles and vegetables are tender, stirring occasionally.

3. Stir in soy sauce and sesame oil; cook 3 minutes. Stir in green onions; ladle into bowls. *Makes 4 servings*

Prep and Cook Time: 20 minutes

quick tip

What's the difference between lo mein and chow mein? The word "mein" simply means noodles in Chinese. Lo mein means tossed noodles; chow mein means fried noodles. Both kinds of noodles are made from wheat flour and egg. The difference is that crispy chow mein noodles are deep fried before using. Ramen noodles can be used in place of Asian curly noodles or lo mein noodles. Just reserve the flavor packet for another use.

szechuan vegetable lo mein

cantonese tomato beef

1 beef flank steak or beef tenderloin (about 1 pound)
2 tablespoons soy sauce
2 tablespoons dark sesame oil, divided
1 tablespoon plus 1 teaspoon cornstarch, divided
1 pound thin noodles
1 cup beef broth
2 tablespoons brown sugar
1 tablespoon cider vinegar
2 tablespoons vegetable oil, divided
1 tablespoon minced fresh ginger
3 small onions, cut into wedges
2 pounds ripe tomatoes (5 large), cut into wedges
1 green onion, cut into thin slices

1. Cut flank steak lengthwise in half, then crosswise into ¼-inch-thick slices. Combine soy sauce, 1 tablespoon sesame oil and 1 teaspoon cornstarch in large bowl. Add beef slices; toss to coat. Set aside.

2. Cook noodles according to package directions. Drain; toss with remaining 1 tablespoon sesame oil. Keep warm. Combine beef broth, brown sugar, remaining 1 tablespoon cornstarch and vinegar in small bowl; set aside.

3. Heat wok or large skillet over high heat 1 minute. Drizzle 1 tablespoon vegetable oil into wok and heat 30 seconds. Add beef mixture and stir-fry 5 minutes or until lightly browned. Remove beef from wok; set aside. Reduce heat to medium. Add ginger and stir-fry 30 seconds.

4. Add remaining 1 tablespoon vegetable oil to wok. Add onion wedges; cook and stir about 2 minutes or until wilted. Stir in half of tomato wedges. Stir broth mixture and add to wok. Cook and stir until liquid boils and thickens.

5. Return beef and any juices to wok. Add remaining tomato wedges; cook and stir until heated through. Serve over cooked noodles.

Makes 4 servings

cantonese tomato beef

nice & spicy

spicy peanut noodle salad

⅓ cup *French's*® Honey Dijon Mustard
⅓ cup reduced-sodium chicken broth
⅓ cup peanut butter
2 tablespoons reduced-sodium teriyaki sauce
2 tablespoons *Frank's*® *RedHot*® Cayenne Pepper Sauce, or more to taste
2 cups thinly sliced vegetables, such as green onion, snow peas, cucumber or bell peppers
4 ounces thin spaghetti, cooked and drained (1½ cups cooked)

1. Combine mustard, chicken broth, peanut butter, teriyaki sauce and *Frank's*® *RedHot*® Sauce in large bowl; whisk until blended.

2. Add remaining ingredients; toss to coat. Serve immediately. If desired, serve on salad greens. *Makes 4 servings*

Tip: To serve as a main dish, add 2 cups diced cooked turkey.

Prep Time: 10 minutes

spicy peanut noodle salad

kung pao chicken

3½ teaspoons cornstarch, divided

5 teaspoons soy sauce, divided

5 teaspoons dry sherry, divided

¼ teaspoon salt

3 boneless skinless chicken breasts (about 1 pound), cut into bite-size pieces

1 tablespoon red wine vinegar

2 tablespoons chicken broth or water

1½ teaspoons sugar

3 tablespoons vegetable oil, divided

⅓ cup salted peanuts

6 to 8 small dried red chiles

1½ teaspoons minced fresh ginger

2 green onions with tops, cut into 1½-inch pieces

1. For marinade, combine 2 teaspoons cornstarch, 2 teaspoons soy sauce, 2 teaspoons sherry and salt in large bowl; mix well. Add chicken; stir to coat. Let stand 30 minutes.

2. Combine remaining 1½ teaspoons cornstarch, 3 teaspoons soy sauce, 3 teaspoons sherry, vinegar, chicken broth and sugar in small bowl; set aside.

3. Heat 1 tablespoon oil in wok or large skillet over medium heat. Add peanuts; cook and stir until lightly toasted. Remove and set aside.

4. Heat remaining 2 tablespoons oil in wok over medium heat. Add chiles; stir-fry until chiles just begin to color, about 1 minute.

5. Increase heat to high. Add chicken mixture; stir-fry 2 minutes. Add ginger; stir-fry until chicken is cooked though, about 1 minute.

6. Add peanuts and onions. Stir cornstarch mixture; add to wok. Cook and stir until sauce boils and thickens.   *Makes 3 servings*

kung pao chicken

hunan chili beef

1 beef flank steak (about 1 pound)
3 tablespoons vegetable oil, divided
3 tablespoons soy sauce
1 tablespoon rice wine or dry sherry
1 tablespoon cornstarch
2 teaspoons brown sugar
1 cup drained canned baby corn
3 green onions, cut into 1-inch pieces
1 small piece fresh ginger (1 inch long), minced
2 cloves garlic, minced
¼ red bell pepper, cut into strips
1 jalapeño pepper,* seeded and cut into thin strips
1 teaspoon hot chili oil
Hot cooked rice

Jalapeño peppers can sting and irritate the skin, so wear rubber gloves when handling peppers and do not touch your eyes.

1. Cut flank steak lengthwise in half, then across the grain into ¼-inch-thick slices. Combine 1 tablespoon vegetable oil, soy sauce, wine, cornstarch and brown sugar in medium bowl. Add beef and toss to coat; set aside.

2. Heat wok or large skillet over high heat 1 minute. Drizzle 1 tablespoon vegetable oil into wok and heat 30 seconds. Add half of beef mixture; stir-fry until well browned. Remove from wok; set aside. Repeat with remaining 1 tablespoon vegetable oil and beef mixture. Reduce heat to medium.

3. Add corn, green onions, ginger and garlic to wok; stir-fry 1 minute. Add red pepper and jalapeño; stir-fry 1 minute.

4. Return beef and any accumulated juices to wok; add chili oil. Cook and stir until heated through. Serve with rice.   *Makes 4 servings*

hunan chili beef

asian pesto noodles

1 pound large raw shrimp, peeled and deveined
    Spicy Asian Pesto (recipe follows)
12 ounces uncooked soba (buckwheat) noodles

1. Marinate shrimp in ¾ cup pesto.

2. Cook soba noodles according to package directions; drain and set aside. Preheat broiler or grill.

3. Place marinated shrimp on metal skewers. (If using wooden skewers, soak in water for at least 30 minutes to prevent burning.) Place skewers under broiler or on grill; cook until shrimp are opaque, about 3 minutes per side.

4. To serve, toss soba noodles with remaining pesto. Serve with shrimp.

Makes 4 servings

spicy asian pesto

3 cups fresh basil leaves
3 cups fresh cilantro leaves
3 cups fresh mint leaves
¾ cup peanut oil
3 tablespoons sugar
2 to 3 tablespoons lime juice
5 cloves garlic, chopped
2 teaspoons fish sauce *or* 1 teaspoon salt
1 serrano pepper,* finely chopped

*Serrano peppers can sting and irritate the skin, so wear rubber gloves when handling peppers and do not touch your eyes.

Combine all pesto ingredients in blender or food processor; blend until smooth.

Makes 2½ cups

asian pesto noodles

cocoa spiced beef stir-fry

2 cups beef broth
3 tablespoons soy sauce
2 tablespoons cornstarch
2 tablespoons HERSHEY'S Cocoa
2 teaspoons minced garlic (about 4 cloves)
1½ teaspoons ground ginger
1 teaspoon crushed red pepper flakes
1 pound boneless top round or flank beef steak
3 tablespoons vegetable oil, divided
1½ cups large onion pieces
1 cup carrot slices
3 cups fresh broccoli florets and pieces
1½ cups sweet red pepper slices
Hot cooked rice
Additional soy sauce
Cashew or peanut pieces (optional)

1. Stir together beef broth, soy sauce, cornstarch, cocoa, garlic, ginger and red pepper flakes; set aside. Cut beef steak into ¼-inch-wide strips.

2. Heat large skillet or wok over high heat about 1 minute or until hot. Drizzle about 1 tablespoon oil into pan; heat about 30 seconds. Add beef strips; stir-fry until well browned. Remove from heat; set aside.

3. Drizzle remaining 2 tablespoons oil into pan; add onion pieces and carrots. Stir-fry until onion is crisp, but tender. Add broccoli and red pepper strips; cook until crisp-tender.

4. Return beef to pan; add broth mixture. Cook and stir until mixture comes to a boil and thickens. Serve over hot rice with additional soy sauce and cashew pieces, if desired.   *Makes 4 to 6 servings*

cocoa spiced beef stir-fry

shrimp in chili sauce

1 pound large raw shrimp, peeled and deveined (with tails on)
1 tablespoon rice wine or dry sherry
4 cloves garlic, minced
1 teaspoon paprika
¼ teaspoon ground red pepper
2 tablespoons water
2 tablespoons ketchup
1 teaspoon cornstarch
½ teaspoon sugar
¼ teaspoon salt
2 tablespoons vegetable oil
1 or 2 jalapeño peppers,* cut into thin slices

Jalapeño peppers can sting and irritate the skin, so wear rubber gloves when handling peppers and do not touch your eyes.

1. Combine shrimp, rice wine, garlic, paprika and red pepper in medium bowl; mix well. Cover; refrigerate 1 to 4 hours.

2. Combine water, ketchup, cornstarch, sugar and salt in small bowl; mix well. Set aside.

3. Heat wok or large skillet over high heat about 1 minute or until hot. Drizzle oil into wok and heat 30 seconds. Add shrimp mixture and jalapeños; stir-fry about 3 minutes or until shrimp turn pink and opaque.

4. Stir cornstarch mixture; add to wok. Cook and stir about 2 minutes or until sauce thickens and coats shrimp. Transfer shrimp to serving dish or individual serving plates. *Makes 4 servings*

shrimp in chili sauce

five-spice beef and bok choy

1 boneless beef top sirloin steak (about 1 pound)
¼ cup soy sauce
2 tablespoons dry sherry
2 teaspoons minced fresh ginger
2 cloves garlic, minced
1 teaspoon sugar
½ teaspoon Chinese five-spice powder*
¼ teaspoon red pepper flakes (optional)
1 large head bok choy
2 teaspoons cornstarch
2 tablespoons peanut oil or vegetable oil, divided
Hot cooked Chinese egg noodles

*Chinese five-spice powder is a blend of cinnamon, cloves, fennel seed, anise and Szechuan peppercorns. It is available in most supermarkets and at Asian grocery stores.

1. Trim fat from beef; discard. Cut beef lengthwise in half, then crosswise into ⅛-inch-thick slices. Combine soy sauce, sherry, ginger, garlic, sugar, five-spice powder and red pepper flakes in medium bowl. Add beef and toss to coat; set aside.

2. Separate bok choy leaves from stems; rinse and pat dry. Stack leaves and cut crosswise into 1-inch slices. Cut stems diagonally into ½-inch slices. Keep leaves and stems separate.

3. Drain beef, reserving marinade. Stir reserved marinade into cornstarch in small bowl until smooth; set aside.

4. Heat wok or large skillet over medium-high heat 1 minute. Drizzle 1 tablespoon oil into wok and heat 30 seconds. Add half of beef; stir-fry 2 minutes or until beef is barely pink in center. Remove beef from wok; set aside. Repeat with remaining beef.

5. Add remaining 1 tablespoon oil and heat 30 seconds. Add bok choy stems; stir-fry 3 minutes. Add bok choy leaves; stir-fry 2 minutes.

6. Stir marinade mixture until smooth; add to wok. Stir-fry until sauce boils for 1 minute and thickens.

7. Return beef and any accumulated juices to wok; cook until heated through. Serve over noodles. *Makes 4 servings*

five-spice beef and bok choy

spicy fried rice with tofu

4 ounces firm tofu, drained
2 eggs
4½ teaspoons vegetable oil, divided
1 tablespoon minced garlic
1 tablespoon minced fresh ginger
½ teaspoon red pepper flakes
2 cups thinly sliced Chinese cabbage
1 cup chopped carrots
1 cup frozen green peas, thawed
3 cups cooked white rice
¼ cup vegetable or chicken broth
¼ cup soy sauce
3 tablespoons dry sherry
2 teaspoons balsamic vinegar

1. Press tofu between paper towels. Cut tofu into ½-inch cubes; set aside.

2. Beat eggs in small bowl with wire whisk. Heat 1½ teaspoons oil in wok or large skillet over medium-high heat. Add beaten eggs; cook and stir 2 to 3 minutes until soft curds form.

3. Remove eggs from wok. Cut eggs into small pieces with spoon; set aside.

4. Heat remaining 3 teaspoons oil in wok over high heat. Add garlic, ginger and red pepper flakes; cook about 30 seconds or until fragrant. Add cabbage, carrots and peas; cook about 5 to 10 minutes until carrots are crisp-tender.

5. Stir in rice, tofu, broth, soy sauce, sherry and vinegar; cook and stir 3 minutes. Stir in eggs just before serving. *Makes 4 servings*

quick tip

When purchasing tofu, check expirations dates. Some brands are refrigerated, others are sold in shelf-stable boxes. Most brands offer a choice of textures—soft, firm or extra firm. After opening, all tofu should be refrigerated, covered with fresh water daily, and used within a week.

spicy fried rice with tofu

seared asian steak salad

¾ **pound boneless sirloin steak (¾ inch thick)**
2 **tablespoons soy sauce**
3 **tablespoons hoisin sauce**
1 **teaspoon freshly grated orange peel**
2 **tablespoons orange juice**
2 **tablespoons cider vinegar**
2 **tablespoons packed dark brown sugar**
2 **teaspoons toasted sesame oil**
1 **teaspoon grated fresh ginger**
⅛ **to ¼ teaspoon red pepper flakes**
1 **bag (5 ounces) spring greens**
½ **cup thinly sliced red onion**
1 **cup thinly sliced red bell pepper**
1 **cup snow peas**
1 **medium carrot, cut into matchstick-size pieces (½ cup)**
 Nonstick cooking spray

1. Place beef and soy sauce in large resealable food storage bag. Seal bag; turn to coat. Marinate beef in refrigerator 2 hours or up to 24 hours, turning several times.

2. Combine hoisin, orange peel, juice, vinegar, sugar, sesame oil, ginger and red pepper flakes in small bowl; set aside. Arrange equal amounts of greens, onion, bell pepper, snow peas and carrots on four dinner plates.

3. Spray large nonstick skillet with cooking spray; heat over medium-high heat. Remove beef from marinade; discard marinade. Add beef to skillet; cook 6 minutes or until desired doneness, turning once. Place beef on cutting board; let stand 3 minutes before thinly slicing.

4. Whisk hoisin mixture until well blended; drizzle over salads. Top each salad with equal amounts of beef. Do not toss. *Makes 4 servings*

seared asian steak salad

pork and red chili stir-fry

1 pound lean boneless pork loin, cut into thin slices

1 teaspoon vegetable oil

2 cloves garlic, minced

¾ pound fresh green beans, cut into 2-inch lengths *or* 1 (10-ounce) package frozen cut green beans, thawed

2 teaspoons sugar

2 teaspoons soy sauce

2 small red chili peppers, thinly sliced *or* ½ teaspoon red pepper flakes

1 teaspoon shredded fresh ginger *or* ½ teaspoon ground ginger

1 teaspoon sesame oil

1 teaspoon rice vinegar

Heat vegetable oil in nonstick skillet. Add pork and garlic; cook and stir until lightly browned. Add green beans; stir-fry until beans and pork are tender, about 5 minutes. Push meat and beans to one side of skillet. Add sugar, soy sauce, chili peppers and ginger; stir to dissolve sugar. Add sesame oil and vinegar. Stir to coat meat and beans. Serve immediately with cooked rice or shredded lettuce. *Makes 4 servings*

Prep Time: 15 minutes

Favorite recipe from **National Pork Board**

quick tip

There are more than 200 varieties of chili peppers, each with its own distinct flavor. The color can be yellow, red, green or black and pepper size varies from a tiny quarter of an inch to a foot long. The heat of chilies can even vary within a variety and comes primarily from the veins and skins. Usually small chilies are hotter than large ones. Hot peppers can sting and irritate the skin, so it's smart to wear rubber gloves when handling them and remember not to touch your eyes.

acknowledgments

The publisher would like to thank the companies and organizations listed below for the use of their recipes and photographs in this publication.

Birds Eye Foods

Bob Evans®

Equal® sweetener

Florida Department of Agriculture and Consumer Services, Bureau of Seafood and Aquaculture

The Hershey Company

National Pork Board

Reckitt Benckiser Inc.

Unilever

metric conversion chart

VOLUME MEASUREMENTS (dry)

⅛ teaspoon = 0.5 mL
¼ teaspoon = 1 mL
½ teaspoon = 2 mL
¾ teaspoon = 4 mL
1 teaspoon = 5 mL
1 tablespoon = 15 mL
2 tablespoons = 30 mL
¼ cup = 60 mL
⅓ cup = 75 mL
½ cup = 125 mL
⅔ cup = 150 mL
¾ cup = 175 mL
1 cup = 250 mL
2 cups = 1 pint = 500 mL
3 cups = 750 mL
4 cups = 1 quart = 1 L

VOLUME MEASUREMENTS (fluid)

1 fluid ounce (2 tablespoons) = 30 mL
4 fluid ounces (½ cup) = 125 mL
8 fluid ounces (1 cup) = 250 mL
12 fluid ounces (1½ cups) = 375 mL
16 fluid ounces (2 cups) = 500 mL

WEIGHTS (mass)

½ ounce = 15 g
1 ounce = 30 g
3 ounces = 90 g
4 ounces = 120 g
8 ounces = 225 g
10 ounces = 285 g
12 ounces = 360 g
16 ounces = 1 pound = 450 g

DIMENSIONS

$\frac{1}{16}$ inch = 2 mm
⅛ inch = 3 mm
¼ inch = 6 mm
½ inch = 1.5 cm
¾ inch = 2 cm
1 inch = 2.5 cm

OVEN TEMPERATURES

250°F = 120°C
275°F = 140°C
300°F = 150°C
325°F = 160°C
350°F = 180°C
375°F = 190°C
400°F = 200°C
425°F = 220°C
450°F = 230°C

BAKING PAN SIZES

Utensil	Size in Inches/Quarts	Metric Volume	Size in Centimeters
Baking or Cake Pan (square or rectangular)	8×8×2	2 L	20×20×5
	9×9×2	2.5 L	23×23×5
	12×8×2	3 L	30×20×5
	13×9×2	3.5 L	33×23×5
Loaf Pan	8×4×3	1.5 L	20×10×7
	9×5×3	2 L	23×13×7
Round Layer Cake Pan	8×1½	1.2 L	20×4
	9×1½	1.5 L	23×4
Pie Plate	8×1¼	750 mL	20×3
	9×1¼	1 L	23×3
Baking Dish or Casserole	1 quart	1 L	—
	1½ quart	1.5 L	—
	2 quart	2 L	—